# The Nauvoo Temple Stone

Written by Timothy Robinson

Illustrated by Robert Barrett

BOOKCRAFT

SALT LAKE CITY, UTAH

*For my great-grandfather*
*Bryant S. Hinckley. One more grateful heart . . .*
*— T R*


*To my family: Elise, Katherine, Blake, Patricia, Anne,*
*Melissa, Brenda, David, Michael, and Eric*
*— R B*

*Library of Congress Cataloging-in-Publication Data*

*Robinson, Timothy M., 1967-*
*Nauvoo Temple stone / written by Timothy M. Robinson ; illustrated by Robert T. Barrett.*
  *p.  cm.*
*Summary: A history of the Nauvoo Temple of the Church of Jesus Christ of Latter-day Saints, from Joseph Smith's*
*founding of Nauvoo, Illinois, in 1839 to the rebuilding of the Temple beginning in 1999.*
  *ISBN 1-57008-776-8 (alk. paper)*
  *1. Nauvoo Temple (Nauvoo, Ill.)--Juvenile literature. [1. Nauvoo*
*Temple (Nauvoo, Ill.) 2. Mormons. 3. Mormon Church--History. 4. Nauvoo*
*(Ill.)]  I. Barrett, Robert, 1949- ill. II. Title.*
*BX8685.N3 R63 2002*
*246'.95'0977343--dc21*                                                  *2001008076*

*Printed in the United States of America*                                *42316-6906*
*Inland Press, Menomonee Falls, Wisconsin*

*10   9   8   7   6   5   4   3   2   1*

In February of 2000, workmen assigned to rebuild the Nauvoo Temple dug up several of the original foundation stones and the stone baptistry drain that had been laid by the Saints back in 1841. They marveled at how smooth, how square, and how carefully crafted they were for stones that would have just been hidden underground. This story is a fictional contemplation of what those workmen might have said.

The workmen gathered their families around to see it. The littlest children squeezed through the forest of grown-up legs and huddled on the ground at their parents' feet.

It took a moment to see it right, even though it was big and the noonday sun was bright, even though it was lying right there where they had pulled it from the earth.

"What is it?" asked one of the children.

"It's just a stone," said another.

"It's not just any stone," said the architect's wife. "It's one of the original stones from the Nauvoo Temple."

"This stone is a testament," said the architect.

"This stone is a prayer," said the surveyor.

"This stone is a monument," said the slab layer.

"This stone is a sentinel," said the foreman.

"This stone is a seed," said the landscaper.

"This stone is a bridge," said the engineer.

The children peered at the stone not sure what to think. The children peered and the stone just sat.

T "This stone is a testament," said the architect. "When the Prophet Joseph Smith first came, this place was a swamp. Crops wouldn't grow because the earth was too soggy. People fell sick with swamp fever and had to be healed by the laying on of hands. But the Prophet stood on this very hill and had a vision of a mighty city with a temple to the Lord.

"They drained the swamp. They built the city. They began work on the temple. They sent men on missions to the north to cut logs and float them down the Mississippi River. They quarried limestone from the earth for the foundation and façade. This stone is one of those limestones. See how smooth and square it is, even after all this time? This stone is a testament to their hard work and industry."

The children reached forward and felt the stone. The children reached forward and the stone just sat.

"This stone is a prayer," said the surveyor. "The Lord told Joseph to build a temple. He told the Prophet that if the people built it, He would make the place holy. He said He would reveal things that had been kept hidden from before the foundation of the world.

"He said He would reveal the ordinances of His priesthood. In the temple, the Saints could make sacred covenants with God. God promised that if they kept His commandments, they could live together with their families forever. Remember the miracles revealed near this stone? This stone is the prayer of a people with faith in the promises of their God."

The children were quiet and listened closely. The children were quiet and the stone just sat.

**T**"This stone is a monument," said the slab layer. "Before the temple was completed, the Prophet and his brother were murdered at Carthage. Wicked men came to Nauvoo with guns and told the Saints that if they didn't leave, they would also be killed."

"Brother Brigham stepped up the work. Every man gave a tenth of his time to building the temple. But the danger was growing and the Saints had to leave. They headed west, but Brigham sent back a team of craftsmen to finish the work and dedicate the temple. Hear how they sacrificed to build it, even though they knew they would have to leave it? This stone is a monument to what they gave up."

The children sighed and shook their heads. The children sighed and the stone just sat.

"This stone is a sentinel," said the foreman. "After the Saints abandoned their homes, mobs came in to destroy the temple. They hauled a cannon up to its doors and fired at targets across the river, shouting and ringing the bell. Looters came to Nauvoo to see what they could find, and what they found was a perfect little town—fences repaired, doors freshly painted—all empty and windswept."

"Not long after, someone set the temple on fire. And a few years after that, a tornado tore down all but its front wall. The ruins lay for years like scattered bones on the ground. Finally someone leveled the land and planted grass. Feel how lonely this stone was in the ground? This stone is a sentinel guarding this spot."

The children looked around at their parents' faces. The children looked around and the stone just sat.

"This stone is a seed," said the landscaper. "From here the Saints moved west over prairies and deserts, until they came to Utah. There they started to build another temple. And then another, and another.

"Now there are more than a hundred temples, all over the world. Imagine how many temples have sprung up from this spot? This stone is a seed planted deep in the earth."

The children all laughed to think of a seed. The children laughed and the stone just sat.

"This stone is a bridge," said the engineer. "It supported a temple right here where we are building another temple. The new temple will look like the old one. The prophet today has called this temple a 'bridge between mortality and immortality.'

"The temple is a place where families are sealed together and promises are made. It's a place where children look to their fathers and fathers look to their children. Do you know about the sealing power of the temple? This stone is a bridge between them and us."

The children looked on and thought of their families. The children looked on and the stone just sat.

But eventually the children left, and the workmen went back to work.

They removed the stone and poured a new foundation. They poured concrete walls and quarried new stone. They placed moonstones, sunstones, and starstones, just as before. They rebuilt the tower with its golden dome. The glass for the windows was poured in an old factory in France, and the window frames were made by hand.

They checked descriptions of the first temple that were written in journals and old newspapers. They studied the original blueprints by William Weeks and a big list of parts called a construction roster. They made the new temple just like the old one.

And when it was finished, another prophet came to dedicate their work. The prophet called it a holy place, where the Lord would reveal mysteries to His people and bless them with His priesthood.

As he spoke the world looked on and saw . . .

a testament, a prayer, a monument, a sentinel, a seed, and a bridge.

But most of all they saw . . .

a temple!

# The Architect's Tale PAGES 6–9

*An architect makes drawings of what a building will look like. She turns ideas into detailed plans.*

When Joseph Smith entered the Nauvoo valley it was called "Commerce," which means money, and it was literally a swamp. But Joseph had a vision of what could be. With the help of William Weeks, an architect, he drew detailed drawings of a city with a temple at its heart. He named the city Nauvoo, which means "beautiful place." Then he went about making it beautiful. To drain the swamp, the Saints dug channels to the river. While they worked, they lived in the few houses that were there and built wooden shacks and lean-tos. Despite their best efforts, many in their company fell ill with malaria—what they called "swamp fever." While some did die, others were miraculously healed by Joseph Smith, Parley Pratt, and others who held the priesthood. In a few years, Nauvoo became a bustling metropolis, the second largest city in the state of Illinois, second only to Chicago. It was filled with beautiful brick homes, a theater, businesses, a "mansion" house, gardens, trees, and, of course, the beautiful temple on the hill that could be seen from the river and for miles around.

# The Surveyor's Tale PAGE 10

*A surveyor is someone who takes careful measurements of the land and records them for everyone else to see.*
*While an architect dreams up what can be, a surveyor sees things as they are.*

In the 124th section of the Doctrine and Covenants, the Lord told Joseph more about how things are in heaven. He taught Joseph about the priesthood, about covenants (like baptism), and why we need temples. Joseph recorded what he learned so we could also learn about it. Some of the most beautiful passages in all of scripture are in D&C 124 and are about the building of the Nauvoo Temple. Among other things, the Lord told Joseph; "And verily I say unto you, let this house be built unto my name, that I may reveal mine ordinances therein unto my people; for I deign to reveal unto my church things which have been kept hid from before the foundation of the world.... If ye labor with all your might, I will consecrate that spot that it shall be made holy.... And again, verily I say unto you, I command you again to build a house to my name, even in this place, that you may prove yourselves unto me that ye are faithful in all things whatsoever I command you, that I may bless you, and crown you with honor, immortality, and eternal life" (D&C 124: 40–41, 44, 55).

# The Slab Layer's Tale PAGES 13–14

*A slab layer uses a crane to pour concrete and set heavy pieces of stone in place—like the granite facing on a temple, or a cemetery monument.*

As Nauvoo grew, Joseph continued sending missionaries out to preach the gospel and tell people about the Book of Mormon. Soon new members began arriving from all over the country and from England and Europe. They all wanted to be near the Prophet and live in Nauvoo. The size and splendor of the city made some people fearful of the Mormons. They told stories that were not true about how the Mormons were secretly trying to take over the state. Soon mobs of angry neighbors came. They attacked the Mormons; some were beaten and even killed. The Prophet Joseph himself was thrown in jail. Joseph pled with the Lord to protect his people (see D&C 120 and 121). But on June 27, 1844, Joseph Smith and his brother Hyrum were shot to death in their prison cell in Carthage, Illinois.

The death of the Prophet was a terrible blow to the Saints. They looked to Brigham Young to know what to do next. More angry people came to Nauvoo and threatened to kill the Saints if they didn't leave. The winter of 1845 was bleak. The Saints knew they would have to leave before spring, and the temple was still not finished. In fact, when Joseph died it was barely past the first floor. The Saints worked very hard and all but completed the temple before leaving the following spring. After the temple was dedicated, some endowments and family sealings were performed there, but many members of the Church would have to wait until the St. George and Salt Lake temples were completed years later before receiving promised temple blessings.

# The Foreman's Tale PAGES 17–18

*A foreman takes orders from the architect and the general contractor and makes sure that things get done.*

Several published accounts by those who visited Nauvoo and the temple in the summer of 1846 told of abandoned homes, unharvested crops rotting in the fields, and broken-down fences. English journalist Charles Lanman recorded that "the very sunshine and the pleasant passing breeze, seemed to speak of . . . sorrow and utter desolation." Colonel Thomas L. Kane recorded that a six-pound cannon was hauled to the temple doors and fired from there at targets across the Mississippi River. After boasting to him of how they had defaced the temple, several drunken men climbed "into the high belfry of the temple steeple and there with the wicked childishness of inebriety, they whooped and shrieked and beat [a drum] that I had seen, and rang in . . . unison their loud-tongued steamboat bell," Kane wrote.

Eventually a fire and a tornado destroyed all but the western wall. For years the temple hill sat in ruin. People took the stones to build other things—some for a school, some for a jail. Farmers tried to use the hill to plant crops, but their plows were bent by the stones left in the ground.

# The Landscaper's Tale PAGE 21

*A landscaper decides what trees and flowers to plant to make the grounds outside of buildings look beautiful. She uses all kinds of seeds for grass, trees, flowers, shrubs, and bushes.*

When the Nauvoo Temple was built the first time, it was only the second temple ever built in the latter days and the first temple where ordinances like baptisms for the dead and endowments were performed. Since then, the Church has built and dedicated over 100 temples. The first few after Nauvoo—St. George, Manti, Logan, and Salt Lake City—were all in Utah, but soon there were temples in Hawaii, Canada, California, and Washington D.C. Now there are temples as far away as Africa, the Philippines, and Japan. Many of these temples have been built just in the last ten years. President Gordon B. Hinckley received a revelation that more temples should be built, including some smaller ones. During the year 2000, a temple was dedicated almost every week, and some weeks as many as seven temples were dedicated. Now members of the Church in places all over the world can be sealed together as families and gain the blessings of the temple.

# The Engineer's Tale PAGE 22

*An engineer is a scientist who studies what makes structures strong. Engineers help the architect determine what kinds of metal or concrete should be used to build strong buildings and other things, such as dams and bridges.*

In the April 1999 general conference, President Gordon B. Hinckley made the exciting announcement that a new temple would be built in Nauvoo where the original temple had stood. This was the fulfillment of a dream for many people, including President Hinckley's own father, Bryant S. Hinckley, who was the mission president in Chicago, Illinois, back in 1939. That was the centennial year for Nauvoo, which means that it had been 100 years since Joseph Smith had founded the city. Bryant Hinckley helped celebrate the centennial by buying back the temple lot for the Church. He asked the leaders of the Church in Salt Lake City to rebuild the temple, but there weren't enough members or enough money at the time to do so. Little could he have known that his own son would someday become a prophet and would help make his vision come true.

# The Rebuilding of the Nauvoo Temple PAGES 23–28

The hard part about building a new temple to look like an old one is figuring out what the old one was really like. There weren't many cameras back in Joseph Smith's day. The pictures they took were called daguerreotypes, and they were grainy and hard to see.

The architects and engineers who rebuilt the Nauvoo Temple were careful to compare their work to the original drawings by William Weeks. They had these drawings because of a little miracle.

In 1948, two missionaries for the Church were in Nauvoo knocking on doors to share the gospel. At one house, they met the grandson of Joseph Smith's architect. This man had some drawings in his basement he wanted to show the missionaries. He thought they might be interested in them.

These drawings turned out to be the original blueprints for the Nauvoo Temple. The man gave the blueprints to the missionaries, and the missionaries gave them to the Church.

Now the builders had the plans to make the new temple just like the old one. The builders hired stone carvers. They carved limestone for the outside of the temple, though the walls of the new temple would be steel and concrete. The carvers also made the starstones, moonstones, and sunstones. These were special decorations that were on the first Nauvoo Temple. To get the design of the sunstones just right, the carvers made a copy of an old sunstone carving that was in a museum. They scanned the copy with lasers to measure it and put the measurements into a computer program. The computer and a special carving machine would help make many more copies of the sunstone for the new temple.

The builders made the new Nauvoo Temple as beautiful as it could be. Once they were finished, the temple was dedicated by a prophet of the Lord.